Brief for Appellants I Case of Milwaukee and Minnesota R.R. Co., vs. Frederick P. James

Anonymous

Brief for Appellants I Case of Milwaukee and Minnesota R.R. Co., vs. Frederick P. James

The Making of Modern Law collection of legal archives constitutes a genuine revolution in historical legal research because it opens up a wealth of rare and previously inaccessible sources in legal, constitutional, administrative, political, cultural, intellectual, and social history. This unique collection consists of three extensive archives that provide insight into more than 300 years of American and British history. These collections include:

Legal Treatises, 1800-1926: over 20,000 legal treatises provide a comprehensive collection in legal history, business and economics, politics and government.

Trials, 1600-1926: nearly 10,000 titles reveal the drama of famous, infamous, and obscure courtroom cases in America and the British Empire across three centuries.

Primary Sources, 1620-1926: includes reports, statutes and regulations in American history, including early state codes, municipal ordinances, constitutional conventions and compilations, and law dictionaries.

These archives provide a unique research tool for tracking the development of our modern legal system and how it has affected our culture, government, business – nearly every aspect of our everyday life. For the first time, these high-quality digital scans of original works are available via print-on-demand, making them readily accessible to libraries, students, independent scholars, and readers of all ages.

The BiblioLife Network

This project was made possible in part by the BiblioLife Network (BLN), a project aimed at addressing some of the huge challenges facing book preservationists around the world. The BLN includes libraries, library networks, archives, subject matter experts, online communities and library service providers. We believe every book ever published should be available as a high-quality print reproduction; printed on-demand anywhere in the world. This insures the ongoing accessibility of the content and helps generate sustainable revenue for the libraries and organizations that work to preserve these important materials.

The following book is in the "public domain" and represents an authentic reproduction of the text as printed by the original publisher. While we have attempted to accurately maintain the integrity of the original work, there are sometimes problems with the original work or the micro-film from which the books were digitized. This can result in minor errors in reproduction. Possible imperfections include missing and blurred pages, poor pictures, markings and other reproduction issues beyond our control. Because this work is culturally important, we have made it available as part of our commitment to protecting, preserving, and promoting the world's literature.

GUIDE TO FOLD-OUTS MAPS and OVERSIZED IMAGES

The book you are reading was digitized from microfilm captured over the past thirty to forty years. Years after the creation of the original microfilm, the book was converted to digital files and made available in an online database.

In an online database, page images do not need to conform to the size restrictions found in a printed book. When converting these images back into a printed bound book, the page sizes are standardized in ways that maintain the detail of the original. For large images, such as fold-out maps, the original page image is split into two or more pages

Guidelines used to determine how to split the page image follows:

• Some images are split vertically; large images require vertical and horizontal splits.
• For horizontal splits, the content is split left to right.
• For vertical splits, the content is split from top to bottom.
• For both vertical and horizontal splits, the image is processed from top left to bottom right.

Supreme Court of the United States.

Nos 231 232 233

MILWAUKEE AND MINNESOTA R R CO
Appellants

vs

FREDERICK P JAMES

Brief for Appellants, the Milwaukee and Minnesota Railroad Company

— COMPLAINANTS —

The bill in this case is filed by Frederick P James a citizen of New York, against the Milwaukee and Minnesota Railroad Company

Bill states that on the 7th day of October 1857, in the District Court of the United States for the District of Wisconsin one Newcombe Cleveland recovered, against the LaCrosse and Milwaukee Railroad Company, judgment for the sum of $111 727 71 and costs.

That the plaintiff by mean assignment, is the owner of said judgment and that the same now remains in force and unsatisfied for the sum of $76 526 39 and interest thereon from November 28 1862

That when said judgment was recovered the LaCrosse Railroad Company owned a railroad known as the La

Crosse and Milwaukee Railroad, extending from Milwaukee to LaCrosse, in two divisions, one from Milwaukee to Portage City, known as the Eastern Division, the other from Portage City to LaCrosse, and known as the Western Division, upon which railroad and appurtenances said judgment became a lien

That subsequently to the entry and docket of said judgment the said LaCrosse Railroad Company on 21st June, 1858, mortgaged said road to William Barnes, in trust to secure bonds for $2,000,000, and a supplementary mortgage to Barnes was made to said Barnes August 11, 1858

That Barnes made a pretended foreclosure of said mortgage and supplement and went through the form of organizing a new corporation under the name of the Milwaukee and Minnesota Railroad Company, and received from Barnes a conveyance of the railroad and all its appurtenances

That the mortgage and supplement to Barnes were fraudulent, for the purpose of delaying and defrauding the creditors of said LaCrosse and Milwaukee Railroad Company, and that the present corporators of the Milwaukee and Minnesota Railroad became such with knowledge of this fraudulent purpose, and that the Milwaukee and Minnesota Railroad Company holds the railroad and its appurtenances in fraud of the creditors of the LaCrosse Railroad Company

States mortgage of Western Division of the road to Bronson Soutter and Knapp, which mortgage was prior to complainant's judgment that said mortgage has been foreclosed, and the lien of complainant's judgment barred

That in latter part of 1857, or beginning of 1858, the LaCrosse Railroad Company became insolvent, and is now, and has no place of business, and has ceased to act as a company.

That Cleveland judgment is a lien on the Eastern Division of said railroad and its appurtenances and complainant has no remedy at law and can only have a remedy in this court

That the Eastern Division is subject to liens prior to complainant's judgment as follows. Mortgage to Palmer, trustee. two mortgages to the City of Milwaukee, mortgage to Bronson and Soutter known as second eastern mortgage and lease and judgment to Chamberlain That these encumbrances amount to $3.500,000

That the Milwaukee and Minnesota Railroad Company is insolvent and has mortgaged said Eastern Division for $600.000, to Scribner and Funda trustees, which mortgage is junior to complainant's judgment lien and that the Milwaukee and Minnesota Railroad Company have diverted the revenues of the road to the payment of principal and interest on said last-mentioned mortgage, and have neglected to keep down interest on the prior incumbrances, but fraudulently diverts the same to complainant's injury

That about October 22, 1857 execution was levied on complainant's judgment upon the LaCrosse Railroad and its property of which the marshal made due return

Prays that complainant's judgment may be decreed to be a lien on said Eastern Division, together with all its property, and that a receiver of said Eastern Division may be appointed, and that he apply the revenue to paying complainant's judgment according to its order of priority. and that said Eastern Division may be sold subject 1st to the Palmer mortgage. 2d the two mortgages to the City of Milwaukee, 3d the mortgage to Bronson and Soutter 4th the lease and judgment to Chamberlain — and that complainant's judgment may be paid

II —DEFENDANT'S ANSWER

Admits Newcombe Cleveland's judgment but does not know amount due on it

Denies that the judgment belongs to complainant, but states judgment really owned by Milwaukee and St. Paul

Company, and that James pretends to own it to uphold jurisdiction in this court

Denies that said judgment was ever a lien on the La Crosse Railroad

States purpose and bona fide character of Barnes mortgage and supplement

Foreclosure and sale of the road under Barnes mortgage, and purchase by Barnes, trustee, and formation of present Milwaukee and Minnesota Railroad Company

Claims right to object to all liens or judgments by La Crosse and Milwaukee Railroad Company with intent to hinder or defraud its creditors

Mortgage to Barnes bona fide

Denies that there has been a valid sale of the Western Division of the road, as said sale has never been confirmed by any court having jurisdiction

That Milwaukee and St. Paul Railroad Company, which pretends to own Western Division is a necessary party, and claims benefit of its non-joinder

Denies that Cleveland judgment ever was a lien on LaCrosse Railroad or the present Milwaukee and Minnesota Railroad

Admits liens on defendant's road 1 Palmer mortgage 2 Two mortgages to City of Milwaukee 3 Mortgage to Bronson and Soutter 4 Mortgage to Scribner and Funda, and no other liens

Denies that Milwaukee and Minnesota Railroad is insolvent

Denies that Milwaukee and Minnesota Railroad Company is diverting revenues of road to payment of Scribner and Funda's mortgage

For years prior to January 1867 defendant's road in charge of a receiver for benefit of Soutter, survivor payment in December, 1866, of $467,000 to Soutter to save road from sale under foreclosure

Fund in court nearly sufficient to pay interest on Bronson and Soutter mortgage and mortgage to City of Milwaukee.

Refusal of St Paul Railroad Company to deliver rolling stock of Eastern Division to defendant and James, the complainant one of the directors of said St Paul Road.

That in consequence of the non-delivery of the rolling stock of Eastern Division great loss has been sustained by defendant

Earnings of road devoted to purchase of necessaries for road

Denies that any proceedings were ever had on Cleveland's judgment to make it a lien on the Eastern Division or its rolling stock &c., and insists it is not a lien on defendant's road

Pleads res judicata as to the questions raised by complainant in regard to Barnes mortgage

Lease to Chamberlain fraudulent, void from want of power in company to make it

Judgment confessed to Chamberlain fraudulent and without consideration.

Cleveland judgment levied among other property, on certain real estate then equitably belonging to La Crosse and Milwaukee Company, describing the same that the interest of the company in said real estate was worth more than the amount of the Cleveland judgment, that by said levy Cleveland acquired a lien and the right thereafter by proper proceedings to have the same applied to the satisfaction of his judgment

That Cleveland afterwards, in October, 1857, filed bill in equity against La Crosse Railroad Company and Chamberlain and court decided that the said real estate was subject to the lien of Cleveland's judgment and ought to be sold to pay the same

That at time said decree was rendered in favor of Cleveland Chamberlain was holding of net revenues of the road more than the amount due on Cleveland's judgment and after the court decided that Chamberlain's judgment was void, Chamberlain bought the Cleveland judgment and obtained control of the suit in equity brought by Cleveland and had the same dismissed as against all the defendants but himself and the La Crosse Railroad Company, and "thus and thereby released the said lands hereinbefore described from the equitable lien created thereon in favor of the Cleveland judgment by the said Cleveland bill and the proceedings thereon, which lands were then held in the names of Kilbourn, Ludington, and Kneeland, defendants to said bill, but really belonged to said company and were of value more than sufficient to pay said judgment." Thence insists that the assignee of the Cleveland judgment cannot enforce his lien against railroad of defendant.

That after Chamberlain dismissed said bill he remained in possession and received from earnings of the road more than enough to pay Cleveland judgment.

Chamberlain when he had more than enough money in his hands to pay Cleveland judgment fraudulently surrendered the road and its appurtenances to Bronson and Soutter, and proceedings were had and a sale under foreclosure ordered of the road, which would have been sold in January, 1866, if defendant had not paid into court $467,000, and but for this payment the road would have been sold and the lien of the Cleveland judgment, if it had a lien, been extinguished.

That Chamberlain now holds over $300,000 and defendant claims that it is entitled to be subrogated to the priority of lien of Bronson and Soutter mortgage, to the amount so by it paid into court aforesaid, and is entitled to retain the railroad until repaid said amount as against the Cleveland judgment (if it be a lien).

That Chamberlain was the owner of the Cleveland judgment, until shortly before institution of this suit, when he pretended to assign the same.

III.—SUPPLEMENTAL BILL.

That sum of $38,000 for interest on the Palmer mortgage, the first lien on the road, became due and remains unpaid and no provision is made by Milwaukee and Minnesota Railroad for its payment

Supplemental mortgage to Palmer, by which the La Crosse and Milwaukee Railroad Company agreed that it would annually set apart from earnings of $12 000 until $200 000 paid, as a sinking fund to retire $500 000 of said bonds and first payment to be made November 1, 1856 that no payments have been made, as provided, to said sinking fund since November 1859, and $72 000 is now due to said fund.

That $40,000 interest on the Bronson and Soutter mortgage, and $11,000 on the mortgage to the city of Milwaukee will be due on September 1, 1860, and that no funds are provided for the payment thereof and the Milwaukee and Minnesota Company do not intend to pay the same

That the Milwaukee and Minnesota Railroad Company have been in possession of the Eastern Division since 9th January, 1866 but have not paid any portion of the interest or principal of the incumbrances on said road that they have not supplied necessaries to said road and are suffering it to go to decay The company has an insufficient force on said road, and is making no permanent improvements on the road, or rolling stock

That if interest be allowed to accumulate, and road and rolling stock to depreciate complainant's security for payment of his debt will become worthless

Complainant fears that if interest, &c , be not paid, foreclosure proceedings will be instituted, and a sale made whereby he will be deprived of all opportunity to collect his judgment

IV —AMENDMENT TO SUPPLEMENTAL BILL

Asks injunction against defendants to prevent their using the railroad

Special prayer for injunction

V.—ANSWER TO SUPPLEMENTAL PILL AND AMENDMENT

Admits about $38,000 has matured for interest on the Palmer mortgage and that a portion of the sinking fund has not been paid

That interest will mature on September 1st next on Bronson and Soutter mortgage, and mortgage given to city of Milwaukee. Denies intention not to pay the same, and intends to pay the same

Large disbursements been made to put road in order, in consequence of the manner in which the same had been managed by the Milwaukee and St Paul Co during the period it had possession, and this while complainant was a director in St Paul Co

Not been able to pay interest on Palmer mortgage but intend to apply earnings as they accrue, that road is in better condition than when received by defendant

Has a sufficient force on the road and necessary repairs made All the outlays necessary made, no greater required than defendant is now making

Believes earnings of road will be equal or nearly so to the payment of interest

No foreclosure proceedings will be had if in the power of Company to prevent it

VI.—DECREE JANUARY 11TH, 1867

1 That the judgment of Newcombe Cleveland against the La Crosse and Milwaukee Railroad Company for $111 727 71 and costs was a lien on the lands, railroad, and appurtenances of the La Crosse and Milwaukee Railroad Company, and that there is now due on said judgment, after deducting payments, $98 801 51

2 That the Milwaukee and Minnesota Railroad Company has succeeded to the property and franchises of the La Crosse and Milwaukee Company, and is subject to the liens thereon

3 That the liens prior to the Newcombe Cleveland judgment are—

A mortgage to Palmer

Two mortgages to the city of Milwaukee

Mortgage to Bronson and Soutter

Judgment in favor of Chamberlain

4 As all the railroad of the La Crosse and Milwaukee Railroad Company, and its other property, excepting 95 miles of railroad from Milwaukee to Portage City, with the rolling stock and appurtenances have been sold on liens prior to the Cleveland judgment, and as that judgment now belongs to complainant it is adjudged that there is due to complainant $98 801 51, and the same is a lien of the date of October 7 1857 on the La Crosse Railroad and its appurtenances from Milwaukee to Portage City.

5 Orders that the railroad known as the La Crosse and Milwaukee railroad, from Milwaukee to Portage City, its depots, station-houses and buildings, together with its rolling stock, franchises and appurtenances, now in the possession of or claimed by the Milwaukee and Minnesota Railroad Company, be sold at public auction by the marshal, unless the defendant prior to such sale pay the amount of complainant's judgment

That the sale be made subject to prior liens of Palmer, Chamberlain and others

That the Milwaukee and Minnesota Company be foreclosed and the purchaser let into possession.

VII —POINTS OF LAW.

From this decree the Milwaukee and Minnesota Railroad Company appeal, and contend that said decree should be reversed or modified on the following grounds

1 It is submitted in limine that the complainant has not shown an assignment of the Cleveland judgment to him in this, that the paper purporting to be such assignment from the St Paul and Milwaukee Railroad Company is not under the seal of the company —(Transcript, p 106)

2

2 That Newton Cleveland having made a levy under his judgment on all the property of the La Crosse and Milwaukee Railroad Company (see statement in the bill Transcript, p 3) the particulars of which levy fully appear in the bill filed by Newcombe Cleveland vs. La Crosse and Milwaukee Railroad Company and others Transcript, p. 47 which statement affects the present complainant was bound to have proceeded with said levy until he had exhausted his legal remedies before applying to the equity jurisdiction of this court

3. That in the case of Newcombe Cleveland v. LaCrosse and Milwaukee Railroad, Selah Chamberlain, and others, the court decreed in favor of Cleveland and sustained his right to be paid out of certain property of the La Crosse and Milwaukee Railroad Company that Selah Chamberlain then became the purchaser of said Cleveland judgment and instead of prosecuting the case to obtain payment of the said judgment, dismissed the bill as against all the defendants but himself and the La Crosse and Milwaukee Railroad Company, which action is binding on the present complainant as claiming through said Chamberlain, and was such laches on the part of Chamberlain as to not entitle the present complainant to the relief prayed

4. It is maintained that if complainant is entitled to any remedy, he must have such remedy as is provided by the laws of Wisconsin, which laws provide for sequestration of the property of corporations and equal distribution among all the creditors

It is submitted that a railroad or its appurtenances cannot, as a matter of course, be sold under execution in Wisconsin, because the statute of Wisconsin, which gives a lien to judgments on land, and renders them subject to sale upon execution, provides for the sale of the franchises of turnpike, plank road, and canal companies "authorized to receive toll for a term of years not absolutely, during

which term purchaser authorized to receive tolls.—(R. S.
1859 ch. 102 sect. 5.)

It appears from this legislation—

(*a*) That the general words authorizing sale under execution in the statute, was not intended to apply to sale of a corporation.

(*b*) The words, authorized to receive "toll," does not apply to railroads.

(*c*.) This further appears from statute passed in 1849, sec. 19, chapter 54 where it is provided that damages recovered for injury done by any corporation "authorized to receive toll, or pay for the transportation of persons or property," may be recovered by warrant of distress.

The revised statutes of Wisconsin, chap. 114, sec. 6, provides that where judgment is obtained against " any corporation," and execution is returned unsatisfied, on petition, the court may sequestrate the corporation and appoint a receiver.

And the court, on final decree, shall cause a fair distribution of the assets "to be made among the fair and honest creditors of such corporation" in proportion to their debts respectively who shall be paid in the same order as provided in case of a voluntary dissolution of a corporation.

In the case of Gelpcke, a judgment creditor, this course was taken by the court.—(Gelpcke v. Horicon R. R., 11 Wiscon. R., 455.)

(*d*) There is a similar statute in Pennsylvania. Under the statute it was held that a judgment creditor could not levy on land used in connection with a canal company, but must proceed by proceedings for sequestration.—(Susquehannah Canal Co. v. Bonham, 9 W. & S., 27.)

In another case in Pennsylvania, the judgment creditor claimed priority, but the court held that he could claim priority out of the tolls collected only, on the ground that his judgment gave him a lien upon them. The road itself could not be taken in execution, citing Ammont v.

The Priest, &c., 13 S. & R. 210, and for the same reason is *not bound by a judgment* —(Leedon v Plymouth R. R. Co., 5 W & S. 265.)

5 What gives force to the view last taken, is that judgments are not liens on railroads, unless there is some special statute so determining

"It has been held that creditors cannot levy their executions upon a turnpike road, and the same rule will necessarily apply to railways'

2 Redfield on Railways, p 626

"It is essential to the existence of a lien that it be recognized by law, by being enforced or protected *as such* This is a very plain principle, and it refuses to a judgment against a municipal corporation the character of a lien Because such a judgment cannot be executed against the land

Shaffer v Cadwallader, 36 Penn R., 129

The Stat of Westm 2 or 13 Edw 1, c 18, gave the elegit which subjected real estate to the payment of debts, and this as a consequence gave a lien on the lands of the debtor

3 Salk, 212

1 Wils, 39

And where there is no statute in a State, which in express terms makes a judgment a lien upon land, the lien, as in England, is the consequence of a right to take out an elegit

United States v. Morrison, 4 Peters 136

The lien depends on the right to sue out an elegit

Bank of U S v Winston's Ex'rs 2 Brock, 252

The lien arises from the power to issue process to subject real estate to the payment of the judgment either by an extension or sale

Massingill v Downs 7 Howard 760

A judgment lien on land only confers a right to levy on the same.

Conard v Atlantic Insurance Co, 1 Peters, 441

A corporate franchise to take tolls on a canal, cannot be seized and sold under a fieri facias, unless authorized by a statute of the State which granted the act of incorporation Neither can the lands or works essential to the enjoyment of the franchise be separated from it and sold under a fi fa. so as to destroy or impair the value of the franchise

> Gue v. Tide Water Canal Co 24 Howard R
> U S , 257

"Where the property cannot be taken in execution there is no lien

> Coombs v Jordan 3 Bland 298

Judgments in Federal Courts owe their quality of being liens to State laws

> Massingill v Downs 7 How , 760
> Williams v. Benedict, 8 How   107
> Bank of Tennessee v Horne, 17 How   157

6 Judgments not being liens on railroads it was very appropriate legislation in the State of Wisconsin to provide a remedy by sequestration, and equal payment to all the creditors

7 It is submitted that even if it be proper to order a sale of the road it should not be made subject to the prior liens, in as much as the judgment to Chamberlain for $629,089 72, one of said apparent liens is seriously controverted on the ground of fraud and was held to be fraudulent by judicial decision in the case of Newcombe Cleveland v La Crosse and Milwaukee Railroad Company, Selah Chamberlain and others, and the sale under such circumstances is not calculated to produce the full value of the property

8 We contend therefore that the decree of the court below should be reversed and judgment rendered in favor of the Milwaukee and Minnesota Company

C CUSHING

APPENDIX

Extracts from Mr Carpenter's Brief in Milwaukee and Minnesota Company vs Chamberlain, No. 181, December Term, 1865

(A) What is the nature of a judgment lien?

In Conrad vs The Atlantic Ins Co, 1 Pet. 443, the court by Story J, say

'Now it is not understood that a general lien by judgment on land constitutes, *per se* a property, or right, in 'the land itself It only confers a right to levy on the "same, to the exclusion of other adverse interest subse-"quent to the judgment and when the levy is actually made on the same the title of the creditor for this purpose relates back to the time of his judgment, so as to "cut out intermediate incumbrances But, subject to "this, the debtor has full power to sell, or otherwise dis-'pose of the land His title to it is not divested or "transferred by the judgment to the judgment creditor. "It may be levied upon by any other creditor, who is en-"titled to hold it against every other person, except such 'judgment creditor and even against him unless he 'consummates his title by a levy on the land under his 'judgment In that event, the prior levy is, as to him, "void and the creditor loses all right under it The "case stands in this respect, precisely upon the same "ground as any other defective levy, or sale The title "to the land does not pass under it In short, a judg-"ment creditor has no *jus in re*, but a mere power to make "its general lien effectual by following up the steps of "the law, and consummating his judgment by an execu-"tion and levy upon the land If the debtor should sell 'the estate he has no right to follow the proceeds of the "sale into the hands of the vendor or vendee or to claim "the purchase money in the hands of the latter. It is 'not like the case where the goods of a person have been 'tortiously taken and sold, and he can trace the pro-'ceeds and waiving the tort chooses to claim the latter. 'The only remedy of the judgment creditor is against "the thing itself, by making that a specific title which 'was before a general lien He can only claim the pro-

"ceeds of the sale of the land when it has been sold on
"his own execution, and ought to be applied to its satis-
"faction'

See also Brace vs Dutchess of Marlborough. 2 P
Wms, 491

This is believed to be the best discussion of the nature
of a judgment lien to be found in the American books
and certainly is clothed with the highest authority.

The lien of the judgment is a right to take the land in
execution nothing more and where for any reason,
whether from express legislative enactment, or the want
of such enactment, or from the nature and character of
the property it can never be sold on execution the judgment is not a lien

Lowry, C J in Schaffer vs Cadwallader, 36 Penn
St, 129, says

"It is essential to the existence of a lien (as of all other
"legal rights) that it be recognized by law by being en-
"forced or protected as such This is a very plain prin-
"ciple, and it refuses to a judgment against a municipal
"corporation the character of a lien because such a judg
'ment cannot be executed against the land

See also Leedom v Plymouth R R 5 W & S, 265
Massingill v. Downs, 7 How, 765

(B) It is understood to be settled that a railroad cannot
be sold on an execution Because it is certain that
franchises cannot be without express legislative sanction
and to authorize the sale of the property of a corporation, without its franchises, would simply ruin every body
and benefit no one

In Winchester T Co vs Vimont 5 B Mon 2, the
Court in reversing a decree which directed the sale of
the road, says

"It can hardly be presumed that a sale of the mere
"road, what the term in common parlance imports, was
"contemplated. It is true the road, consisting of a nar-
"row strip of ground, between Winchester and Lexing-
"ton, with a partial covering of rock upon it, belongs to
"the company but only for particular uses and purposes

" As to the land, the company has merely a right of way
' over it, for the road, for its construction and continu-
" ance It can be used for no other purpose, and when
' it shall cease to be so used, it will revert to the donors or
" grantors thereof to the company The purchaser,
" therefore, would acquire nothing, which he could ren-
" der available and productive, unless the corporate power
" of the company would follow or be included in the sale
' of the road But it is evident this would not be the
" case The power for the control and management of
' the road, according to the provisions of the charter is
' vested in the owners of the stock, which they exert
" through the officers whom they are authorized to ap-
' point This power would not be acquired by the pur-
" chaser, as the stock is not to be sold The acquisition
" of the purchaser, therefore, would not enrich him, but
' would render the company poor indeed. The corpora-
' tion would not only then be as corporations are said to
' be without a soul but it would thereby be without sub
' stance The inevitable effect of such a sale would be
" to destroy the road and the corporation It would be
' a useless, ruinous, and unnecessary sacrifice of private
" interest and tend to the destruction of a cherished ob-
" ject of public interest and convenience '

See also Leedom v Plymouth R. R Co , 5 W & S , 265
　　　　Ammant v President, &c , 13 Serg & R., 210.
　　　　Susquehanna Canal v Bonham. 9 W & S , 27
　　　　Sermour v. The Mitford. &c , 10 Ohio, 480.
　　　　McLean J. Coe v. Hart, 6 Am Law Reg , 41
　　　　Ludlow v. Hurd 6 Am Law Reg., 502
　　　　Tippetts v Walker 4 Mass , 596
　　　　Redfield on Railways 606
　　　　Covington Bridge v Shepherd, 21 How , 112.
　　　　Gue v Tide Water Co , 24 How , 262

Liens of judgments exist only by force of statutory
provisions, and are not to be extended by implication.
(Isaacs v Swift, 10 Cal., 71.)

In Douglas v Huston, 6 Ohio, 162, the court say

' The existence, validity, and extent of a judgment
' lien in this State are matters purely legal dependent

'upon statutory provisions; and if the lien fails at law
' it cannot be aided in equity

See also Buchan vs Sumner, 2 Barb, Ch 193, and
Mower v Kip, 6 Paige, 88, holding that the Court of
Chancery will give effect to the lien of a judgment only
so far as it could have been enforced at law.

In Coombs v Jordan, 3 Bland 298, the Chancellor
says

'This judgment lien is a uniform consequence of the
"real estate being liable to be taken and extended under
"an execution issuing upon such judgment Wherever,
then, such a liability exists the lien arises as the con-
stant incident of such a judgment and where the pro-
"perty cannot be taken in execution there is no lien It
' will, therefore, be sufficient in this, or any similar case
' to shew the liability of the real estate to be so taken in
"execution to establish the existence of the lien '

See also Dosier vs Lewis, 27 Miss, 679
Corwin vs Benham, 2 Ohio, (N S) 36

(C) Judgments rendered in the federal courts owe
their quality of being liens solely to State statutes
Massingill v. Downs 7 How 760
Williams v Benedict, 8 How , 107
Bank of Tennessee v Horn, 17 How , 157

(D) The statute of Wisconsin, R S 1859 ch 102 , sec
5 provides " All judgments hereafter rendered in any
court of record shall bind, and be a charge upon lands,
"tenements, real estate and chattels real, in every county
' where the record, &c , and such estate and chattels
"real shall be subject to be sold upon execution to be
"issued on such judgment '

The phraseology of this statute shows that it was not
intended to include a railroad and franchises, it contains
no term that can be construed to embrace franchises

This is further manifest from the fact that the same
statute (Ch 54, sec 11, &c) provides for the sale of the
franchises and property of turnpike, plank road and canal

3

companies companies ' authorized to receive toll,' not
in fee to the highest bidder for a certain sum, as real
estate and chattels real are to be sold under chapter 102,
but for a term of years, by which the purchaser becomes
authorized ' to receive during that time all such ' toll as
the said corporation would by law be entitled to demand "

The latter statute is conclusive of two things

(1) The Legislature did not understand chapter 102,
sec 5, as applying to the property and franchises of any
corporation and—

(2) The Legislature did not intend to authorize the
sale of railroads on execution for they are not included
in the latter statute upon a kindred subject

The word tolls means not the sums collected by a company for the transportation of freight or passengers, but
taxes paid for some liberty or privilege, " particularly for
the privilege of passing over a bridge or on a highway,'
&c — *Webster*.

(E.) Some of the earlier railroad charters in this coun-
try contemplated the construction of a road, to be used by
the public, paying toll for passage as turnpikes are used,
and some of the earlier charters provide, as a separate
grant, that the company may also transport passengers
and property over its own road thus providing for a
joint use of the road by the company and the public

But this railroad company (and the remark is believed
to be true of all the later railroad charters, especially in
Wisconsin), was not authorized to build a road to be used
by the public on payment of tolls Its grant of power
is to build a railroad, and to " transport take, and carry
" property and persons upon said road by the power and
" force of steam,' &c

The Revised Statutes of Massachusetts, (1836,) Ch
44, provide as follows

" Sec 12. When any judgment shall be recovered
" against any turnpike or other corporation authorized to
' receive toll, the franchises of such corporation, with all

" the rights and privileges thereof. so far as relates to the
" receiving of toll, and also all other corporate property,
" real and personal, may be taken on execution or war-
' rant of distress and sold by public auction

' Sec 13 The officer to give notice of sale &c

" Sec 14 The officer may adjourn sale &c.

" Sec 15 In the sale of the franchise of any corpora-
" tion, the person who shall satisfy the execution or war-
" rant of distress, with all legal fees and expenses thereon,
" or who shall agree to take such franchise for the short-
" est period of time and to receive during that time all
" such toll as the said corporation would by law be enti-
" tled to demand shall be considered as the highest bid-
" der

' Sec 16. The officer's return on such execution shall
' transfer to such purchaser all the privileges and immu-
' nities which by law belonged to such corporation so far
" as relates to the right of demanding toll and the offi-
" cers shall immediately after such sale, deliver to the
" purchaser possession of all the toll houses and gates
" belonging to such corporation, in whatever county the
' same may be situated and the purchaser may there-
' upon demand and receive all the toll which may accrue
' during the time limited by the terms of the purchase,
" in the same manner and under the same regulations,
' as such corporation was before authorized to demand
' and receive the same '

"Section 17 ' Purchaser to have action for disturbance
of franchise &c

Section 18 The corporation to continue in all other
respects clothed with same powers, bound to same duties,
&c , as though no sale had taken place

Section 19 Such corporation "may redeem, &c

"Section 20 Whenever any damages have been, or
" may hereafter be assessed in favor of any person either
" by an order of county commissioners, or by the verdict
" of a jury for any injury sustained in his property, by
" the doings of such turnpike, or other corporation au-
' thorized to receive toll, and the said damages shall re-
" main unpaid, for the space of thirty days after such
' order or verdict, such person may have a warrant of
' distress against such corporation, for the damages as-
" sessed, together with the interest thereon, and his rea-
" sonable costs

This statute provided for two cases

(1) The collection of judgments

(2) The collection of the value of lands taken, and other injuries occasioned to land owners by the location and construction of such public work, after the same had been assessed according to law.

But the remedy given in both instances was confined to turnpike and other corporations authorized to receive toll, and did not apply to railroads

The Legislature of Massachusetts in 1847 (Chap 259) made a similar provision as to railroads, in case of unpaid assessments, as follows

"Section 3. Whenever damages shall have been as-
' sessed against any railroad corporation, upon the peti-
'tion of any person injured by the location and con-
"struction of their road, by the county commissioners, or
"the verdict of a jury said commissioners may issue
"warrants of distress to compel the payment of such
"damages together with costs and lawful interest *Pro-
"vided* that no such warrant shall issue till after the
"expiration of the time allowed by law for filing a peti-
"tion for a jury '

In Massachusetts, after the assessment of damages in favor of land owner, an appeal may be taken to the common pleas, where a jury assesses the damages These proceedings may be reviewed by the Supreme Court on bill of exceptions, but when the amount is ascertained, it is certified by the Supreme Court to the commissioners, and they issue distress warrant under this statute

Com. v Boston & M R R Co, 3 Cush 57.

(F) In the revision of the statutes of Wisconsin of 1849, sections 12, 13, 14, 15, 16, 17, 18 19, of the Massachusetts Revised Statutes are substantially adopted, and are sections 11, 12, 13, 14, 15, 16, 17, and 18, of Wisconsin, Chapter 54

But the Legislature wishing to adopt the amendment made in Massachusetts, before cited, passed the 20th section of the Massachusetts Revised Statutes, the 19th of Wisconsin, as follows

'Section 19. Whenever any damages may have been "or may hereafter be assessed, in favor of any person, "for injury sustained in his property by the doings of 'any such turnpike, or other corporation authorized to 'receive toll, or pay for the transportation of persons 'and property, and the said damages shall remain unpaid "for the space of thirty days after such assessment, such "person may have a warrant of distress against such cor-"poration for the damages assessed, &c '

The Legislature of Wisconsin in order to give a remedy by warrant of distress for unpaid damages assessed, as well against railroad companies, as turnpike and other corporations authorized to receive toll, as had been done by the act of 1847 in Massachusetts to accomplish their purpose, after the words "turnpike or other corporation authorized to receive toll, ' in the original section added the words "or pay for the transportation of persons and property, ' not found in the original section.

This is conclusive to show that the mind of the Legislature was directed to this precise point, and from the fact that in the case where they wished to include railroad they employed for that purpose words not found in the parent statute, the conclusion is irresistible that in the provisions in relation to judgments the Legislature of Wisconsin did not design to include railroads because they adhered to the precise language of the parent sections in that behalf Had it been the purpose of the Legislature of Wisconsin to permit railroads as well as turnpikes to be sold on execution the same words which were inserted in section 19 would also have been inserted in the sections relating to judgments

(G) The same Revised Statutes of Wisconsin made the following general provisions for collecting judgments against all corporations

Chap 114, "Sec 6 Whenever a judgment at law, or " decree in chancery, shall be obtained against any corpo-

" ration, incorporated under the laws of this State, and
" an execution issued thereon shall have been returned
' unsatisfied in whole or in part, upon the petition of the
" person obtaining such judgment or decree, or his repre-
" sentatives, the Circuit Court within the proper county
" may sequestrate the stock, property, things in action,
" and effects of such corporation, and may appoint a re-
' ceiver of the same

"Sec 7 Upon a final decree upon any such petition, the
" court shall cause a just and fair distribution of the
" property of such corporation, and of the proceeds there-
" of, to be made among the fair and honest creditors of
" such corporation, in proportion to their debts respect-
" ively, who shall be paid in the same order as provided
' in the case of a voluntary dissolution of a corporation "

Gelpcke vs. The Horicon Railroad, reported, on collat-
eral questions 11 Wis 455, was a proceeding under this
statute

The order of sequestration in the Court below, recited
that Gelpcke, a judgment creditor, whose execution had
been returned unsatisfied, had presented to said · Court,
a petition, in the form of a complaint against the defendant the Milwaukee and Horicon Railroad Company.'
setting forth &c, and proceeded, "and the Court having
duly considered the same, the Court does here order, ad-
judge and decree in · pursuance of Chapter 148 of the
Revised Statutes of this State' (being the R S 1858,
the same as Chapter 114 R S 1849, before cited) ' that
the stock, property real and personal, things in action
and effects of said corporation of whatever name, nature
and description, be and the same are hereby sequestrated
for the benefit of all the creditors of said corporation,"
and appointed a Receiver of the property, franchises, revenues, &c, of the company, with authority to operate
the road, &c

This is cited to show that this statute is regarded by
our State Courts as furnishing the proper remedy against
railroad companies.

This statute gives no preferences not even in favor of the judgment upon which the sequestrating proceeding is instituted   The final decree is to distribute the property of the corporation among all the fair and honest creditors of the corporation, not in the order of the dates of their judgments, but ' in proportion to their debts respectively

(H) In connection with the provision before quoted from other chapters of the statute, the effect is to give the creditor of a railroad company exactly the same remedies enjoyed in Pennsylvania against all corporations   After the decisions in Amant vs The Prest &c , 13 S & R 210, in which the Court held that the road could not be sold, and where the Chief Justice suggested that the Legislature ought to provide a remedy by sequestration, the following statute was enacted.

Act of June 16, 1836

"LXXII   All executions which shall be issued from " any Court of Record, against any corporation not being "a County, Township or public corporate body, shall " command the sheriff or other officer to levy the sum " recovered together with the costs of suit of the goods " and chattels, lands and tenements of such corporations " and such execution shall be executed in the manner fol- " lowing, to-wit

' 1   The officer charged with the execution of such " writ, shall go to the banking houses or other principal " office of such corporation, during the usual office hours, "and demand of the president, or other chief officer, ' cashier, treasurer, secretary, chief clerk or other officer, " having charge of such office, the amount of such exe- ' cution, with legal costs

" 2   If no person can be found, on whom demand can " be made, as aforesaid, or if the amount of such execu- "tion be not forthwith paid, in lawful money, after de- "mand as aforesaid, such officer shall seize personal " property of said corporation, sufficient to satisfy the " debt, interest and cost, as aforesaid

' 3   If the corporation against which such execution " shall be issued, be a banking company and other suf-

"ficient personal property cannot be found, such officer
"shall take so much of any current coin of gold, silver
"or copper which he may find, as shall be sufficient to
"satisfy the debt interest and cost, as aforesaid

"4 If no sufficient personal property be found as
"aforesaid, such officers shall levy such execution upon
"the real estate of such corporation, and thereupon, pro-
'ceed in the manner provided in other cases, for the sale
'of land upon execution

"LXXIII In every case in which judgment shall
"have been obtained against such corporation except as
"aforesaid, and an execution issued thereon shall have
"returned, unsatisfied, in part or in whole, it shall be
'lawful for the Court in which such judgment shall have
·been obtained, upon the bill or petition of the plaintiff
"in such judgment, to award a writ to sequester the
"goods, chattels and credits rents, issues and profits,
"tolls and receipts from any road canal bridge or other
"work, property or estate of such corporation

"LXXIV. The court shall, upon the awarding of any
"such writ, appoint a sequestrater to execute the same,
"and to take charge of the property and funds taken or
"received by virtue of such writ, and to distribute the
'net proceeds thereof among all the creditors of such
"corporation, according to the rules established in the
"case of the insolvency of individuals, and such seques-
"trater shall have all the powers and be subject to all the
'duties of masters appointed under the law relating to
"insolvent debtors." &c

(I) Under this statute the Court in Susquehanna Canal
Co. vs Bonham, 9 W. & S, 27, held that the creditor
could not levy upon any land used in connection with the
road, as for toll-houses and gates. The Court say

'The remedy for creditors in such case by sequestra-
'tion was suggested in the opinion of Chief Justice
'Tilghman, (13 Serg & Rawl., 310,) and has since been
"carried into effect by the provisions of the act of 16th
"June, 1836, and it gives to the creditor all the redress
"the Legislature thought he could have against the pro-
"perty necessary to the company, consistent with the pre-
"servation of the public interests"

See also Redfield on Railways, 606

Mann vs Pentz, 3 Comstock, 415.

Leedon vs The Plymouth R R Co , 5 W & S. 265, was a case of sequestration under this statute where Leedon, the plaintiff, a judgment creditor who had instituted the proceedings claimed priority in favor of his judgment. The Court say

"The plaintiff could claim a priority out of the tolls "collected only on the ground that his judgment gave "him a lien upon them. To have this effect he must "make out that these tolls were such an interest in land "existing in the corporation at the time when the judg-"ment was rendered as to be bound by it. The road "itself could not be taken in execution (Ammont vs "The President, &c , 13 S & R , 210 and for the same "reason is not bound by a judgment, much less is the "right of taking tolls from the passengers and freighters, "which is a corporate franchise, a species of incorporeal "hereditament incident to the road —(2 Black. Com , "38) These tolls were all collected after the judgment "rendered and after the appointment of the sequestra-'ter. The effect of the 74th section of the act of 16th 'June, 1836, relating to executions which adopts the "provisions of the 27th section of the act of 16th June, "1836, relating to insolvent debtors is merely to save 'the judgment, mortgage and execution creditors then 'liens existing at the time of the sequestration. The 'plaintiff has none such here to receive the protection of "the act.

(K) Independent of statutory provisions, the only remedy of a judgment creditor is to exhibit his bill in equity, and thus and thereby create an equitable lien upon the revenues of the road —(Covington Bridge v Shepherd, 21 How , 112) But where there is a statute like the one last-above quoted, providing a remedy by sequestration, it is submitted that such remedy is exclusive of all others. However this may be it is certain that in regard to the Cleveland judgment now under consideration, no proceedings whatever, either under the statute or in equity, had fixed a lien upon the revenues of the debtor company, and in 1859, on the foreclosure of the Barnes mortgage, the property passed to the Milwaukee and Minnesota Company, (Bronson v. R. R., 2 Wallace, 304,) and it is now too late for any proceedings whatever to make that judgment a lien

(L.) If the court shall hold that judgments at law are not liens upon railroads, as we have claimed under the last point, then this bill will fail so far as regards the cancellation of the Cleveland judgment, because if that judgment is not a lien the Milwaukee and Minnesota Company has no interest in having it cancelled

But in that event the bill must be sustained for the purpose of enforcing an accounting as to the revenues received by Chamberlain after the foreclosure of the Barnes mortgage and the vesting of the property in the Minnesota Company